W9-BCS-930

THE NEW CREEPY CRAWLY COLLECTION

SCORPIONS

For a free color catalog describing Gareth Stevens' list of high-quality books and
multimedia programs, call 1-800-542-2595 (USA) or 1-800-461-9120 (Canada).
Gareth Stevens Publishing's Fax: (414) 225-0377.
See our catalog, too, on the World Wide Web: http://gsinc.com

Library of Congress Cataloging-in-Publication Data

Green, Tamara.
  Scorpions / by Tamara Green ; illustrated by Tony Gibbons.
    p. cm. -- (The New creepy crawly collection)
  Includes bibliographical references (p. 24) and index.
  Summary: Describes the physical characteristics, habitat, and behavior of scorpions,
as well as miscellaneous information about these members of the spider family.
  ISBN 0-8368-1580-7 (lib. bdg.)
  1. Scorpions--Juvenile literature. [1. Scorpions.] I. Gibbons, Tony, ill. II. Title. III. Series.
QL458.7.G74 1996
595.4'6--dc20   95-54172

This North American edition first published in 1996 by
Gareth Stevens Publishing
1555 North RiverCenter Drive, Suite 201
Milwaukee, Wisconsin 53212 USA

This U.S. edition © 1996 by Gareth Stevens, Inc. Created with original © 1995 by
Quartz Editorial Services, 112 Station Road, Edgware HA8 7AQ U.K.

Additional illustrations by Clare Heronneau.

Consultant: Matthew Robertson, Senior Keeper, Bristol Zoo, Bristol, England.

All rights reserved. No part of this book may be reproduced, stored in a retrieval system,
or transmitted in any form or by any means, electronic, mechanical, photocopying, or
otherwise, without the prior written permission of the copyright holder.

Printed in Mexico

1 2 3 4 5 6 7 8 9 99 98 97 96

THE NEW

CREEPY CRAWLY
COLLECTION

SCORPIONS

by Tamara Green
Illustrated by Tony Gibbons

Gareth Stevens Publishing
MILWAUKEE

Contents

Getting to know
scorpions

If you ever go camping in warm parts of the world, be sure to watch out. Creatures called *scorpions* might just be around. They have a habit of crawling into shoes and sleeping bags, and some have a poisonous sting. So be careful not to step or lie down on a scorpion and make it angry. It might just get its revenge!

In all, there are about 650 different types of scorpions. Some are tiny — only 1/5 inch (1/2 centimeter) long; others can be 8 inches (20 cm) long.

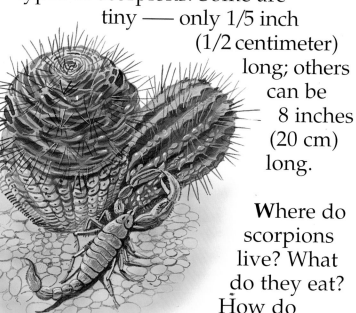

Where do scorpions live? What do they eat? How do they mate?

Where is their stinger? Do they always attack? What is likely to happen if they do?

Read on and learn about these extraordinary nocturnal creatures that can sometimes prove fatal to humans.

Body talk

It's not easy to spot scorpions in the wild because they mostly move around by night. Even then, they will usually be aware of your approach. They will rush to hide in the nearest hole, beneath a piece of tree bark or maybe under some dead leaves.

Scorpions certainly look scary. And, by nature, they often live up to their appearance. Some of them, as you will find out later in this book, can kill humans with their sting. Scorpions can also be hostile to one another in certain situations. They can even be cannibalistic.

Scorpions, like spiders, have eight legs and belong to the *arachnid* family. As you can see in this illustration, their bodies are divided into segments, and they have a pair of large claws, much like a lobster's claws.

The largest scorpions are usually dark in color, and smaller ones are paler.

The scorpion's entire body is covered with a tough coating. In many ways, this acts like a soldier's armor.

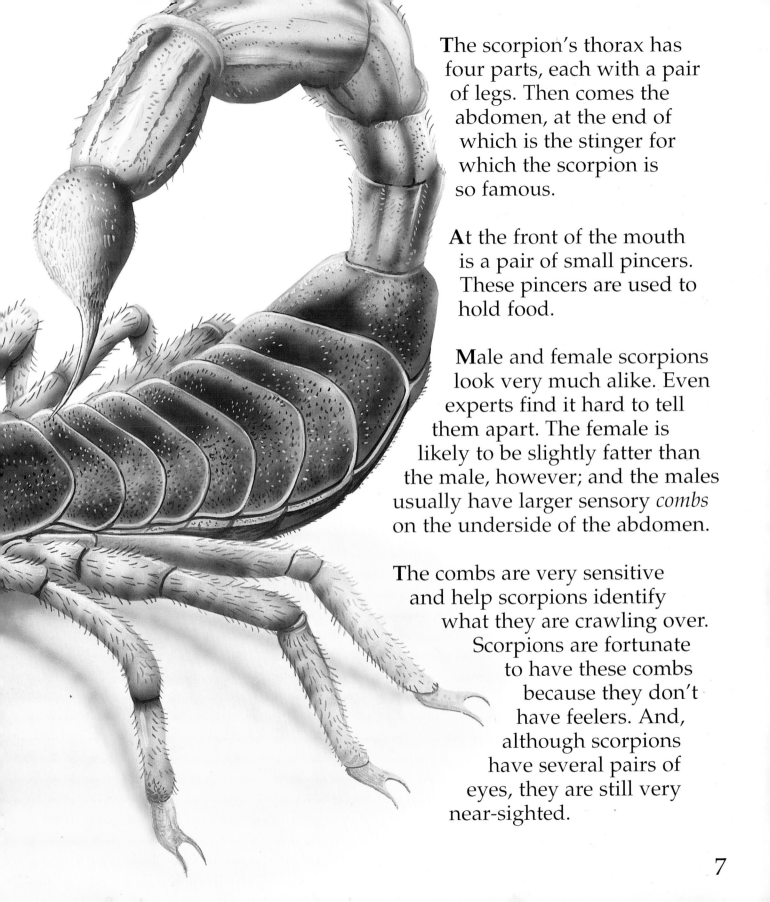

The scorpion's thorax has four parts, each with a pair of legs. Then comes the abdomen, at the end of which is the stinger for which the scorpion is so famous.

At the front of the mouth is a pair of small pincers. These pincers are used to hold food.

Male and female scorpions look very much alike. Even experts find it hard to tell them apart. The female is likely to be slightly fatter than the male, however; and the males usually have larger sensory *combs* on the underside of the abdomen.

The combs are very sensitive and help scorpions identify what they are crawling over. Scorpions are fortunate to have these combs because they don't have feelers. And, although scorpions have several pairs of eyes, they are still very near-sighted.

7

Where in the

Scorpions sometimes turn up in unexpected places — southern England, for example, where most types are not found naturally. That's probably because they crept into someone's luggage or into a crate of imported tropical fruit.

Most scorpions like warmth. They are usually found in desert areas.

Deserts such as the African Sahara, Arizona's desert, and the Australian outback — all provide ideal habitats for scorpions. They also like to live in rain forests, such as those in South America. To avoid the excessive heat of the day, they burrow into the ground or hide under stones. But scorpions have another way of cooling down when it is too hot for comfort.

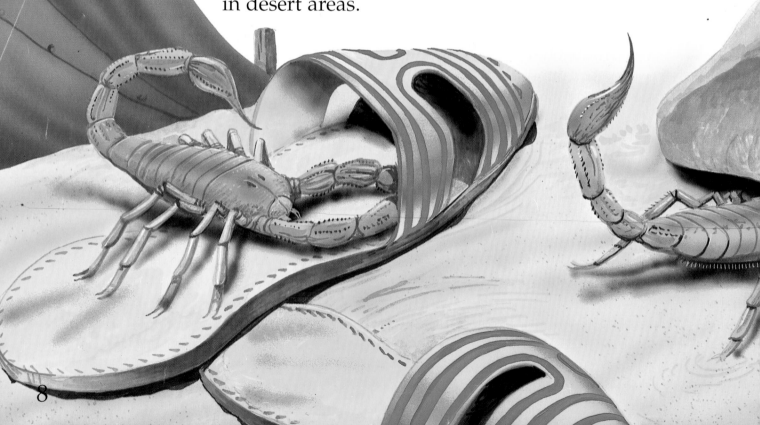

world?

They straighten their legs and stand so their bodies do not touch the ground, as you can see in the illustration below. This allows more air to circulate around their bodies, and this lowers their temperature quite a bit.

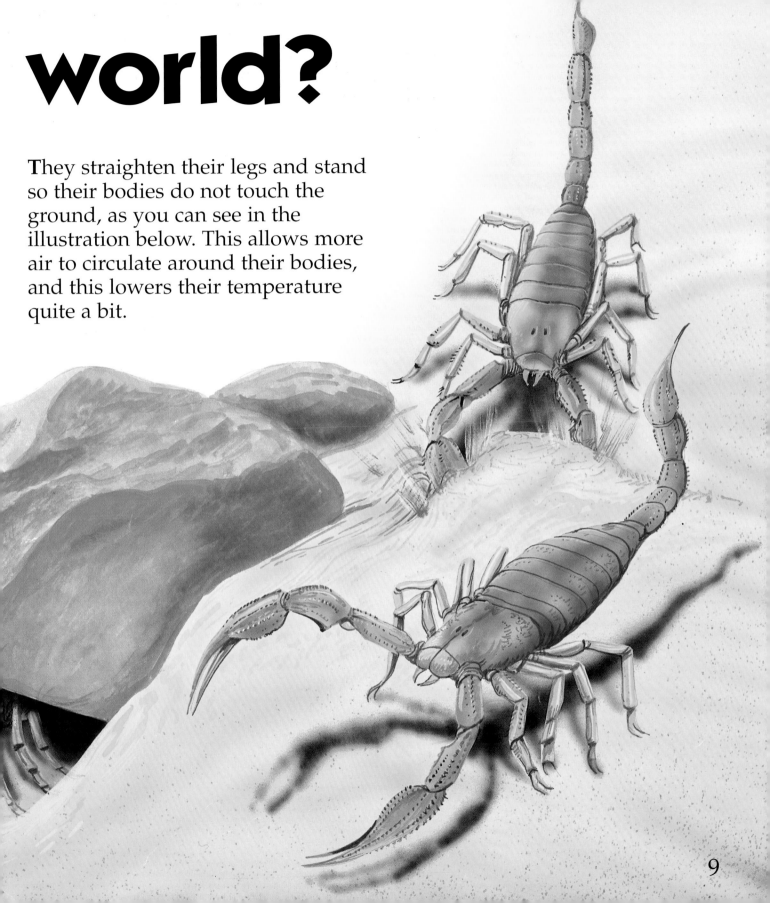

Finding a mate

Scorpions are usually solitary creatures, living alone rather than in colonies. As a result, both males and females are fortunate if they manage to find a mate at all.

When they do, however, it's not always instant attraction. First, a complicated courtship ritual takes place. The male faces the female, and then grasps her claws with his claws. At this point, it looks as if they are having fun and dancing together!

But if the female resists his advances, the male may threaten her with his sting. She is just as clever, though, and may threaten him back with hers.

Once the female is in his grasp, the male then drags the female to a suitable area for mating.

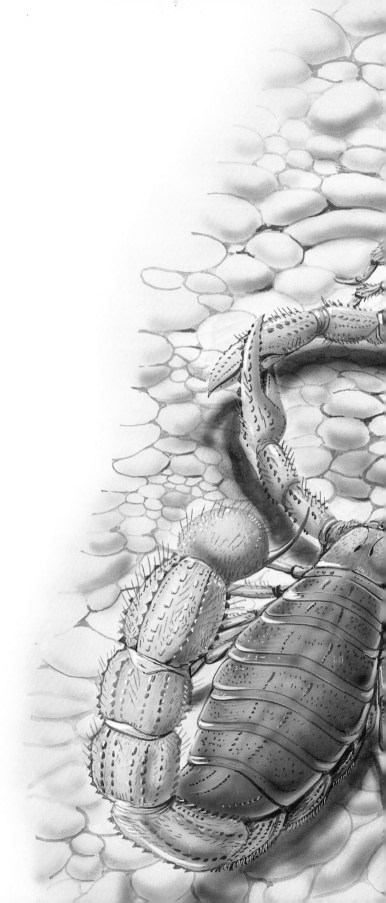

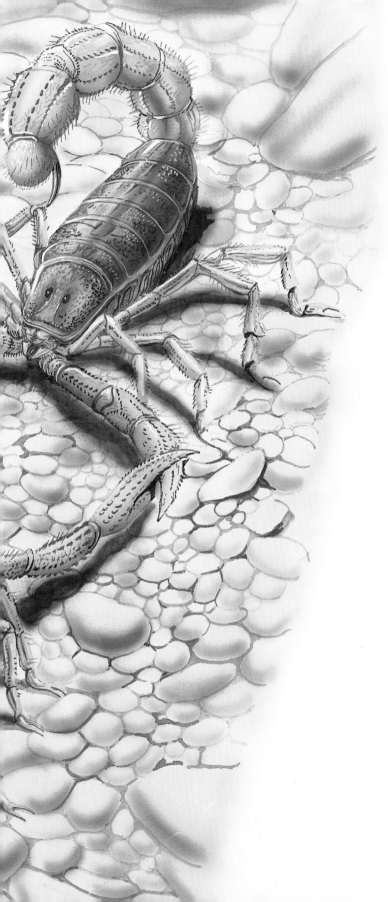

Next, the male scrapes the soil with his feet and makes a hollow. Here, he deposits sperm, which the female collects. At this point, the female may actually devour the male — not a kind way to treat the father of her babies! But she does get a nutritional meal to help her produce strong offspring.

Young scorpions do not hatch from eggs, but are born alive a few weeks later. When scorpions are born, they are less than one-eighth the size of their mother, but look just like her. They are born inside a skin covering that the mother breaks open with her stinger to release the babies. They now climb onto their mother's back and ride around this way until they are able to look after themselves. Sometimes a mother scorpion has so many young ones on her back that she looks furry.

The young are colorless at first and not very strong, so they sometimes fall off their mother's back. They grow quickly, however, and molt, or shed, about seven times before they reach adult size.

Nighttime

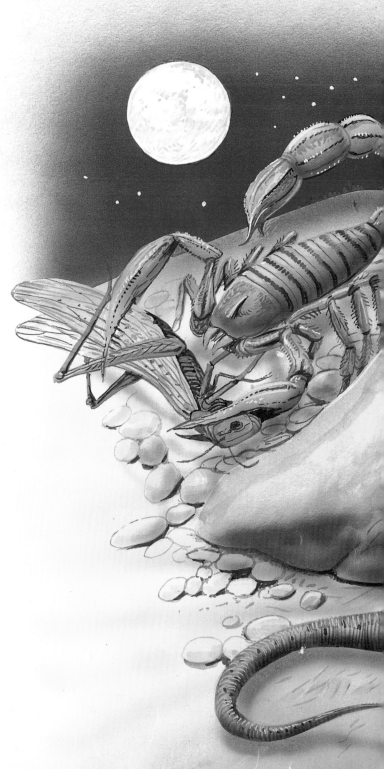

Scorpions are greedy by nature and may occasionally spring out during daylight to catch a passing insect from a burrow entrance. But most scorpions hunt at night, and they generally avoid the light of day. In darkness, the scorpions see even less well than during the day, but they are highly skilled at picking up vibrations through their touch-bristles and can sense the approach of a juicy meal.

Their claws are ideal for holding onto victims, and the small pincers at the front of their mouths are well suited for grasping, as well. Only if they meet with resistance will they actually sting their meal.

It is not so much their victims' flesh that scorpions are interested in, however. It is body fluids they seek. In fact, scorpions drink much more than they eat!

hunters

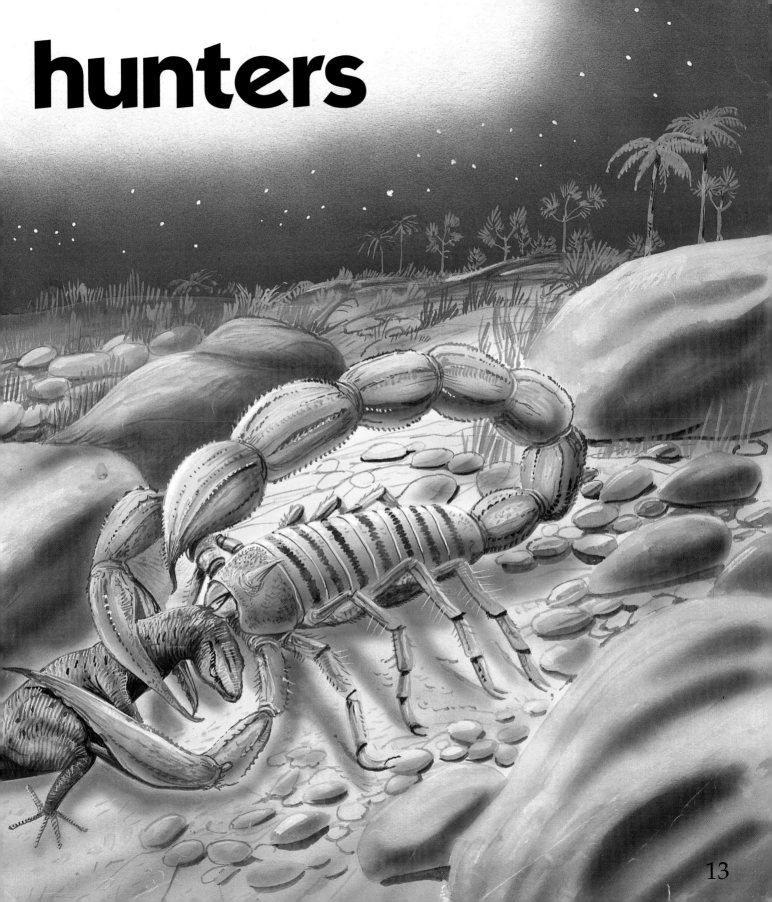

Tail

A young boy collapses. Lying there, sweat pouring from his face and body, he suddenly finds it difficult to breathe and begins to vomit. His limbs go numb, and he can hardly feel them. Then, all of a sudden, he starts foaming at the mouth.

There is no time to lose! He must be rushed to a hospital while there is still a chance doctors may be able to treat him and save his life. He has been stung by one of the most venomous scorpions of all.

Unfortunately, humans do not have good enough hearing to recognize the peculiar sound made by the desert creature as a warning. The scorpion had been rubbing part of its body against one leg to produce an odd purring noise, but the boy was unaware of this.

14

stingers

Not all scorpions will sting to the death in this way. In fact, most are only dangerous if annoyed or provoked. Many scorpion stings are no more dangerous than wasp stings. But some can be fatal, so beware.

When a scorpion is angry, it holds out its pincers and curves its tail right over its back, ready to stab a victim with its stinger.

The tip of the stinger carries the venom. Two large glands supply the stinger with venom.

This may seem hard to believe but, in some warm countries, including the United States, more people die from scorpion stings in any one year than from snake bites.

Duel to

The South American camel spider struck a threatening pose in the sand. It was a savage carnivore measuring just 6 inches (15 cm) across.

This awesome-looking camel spider was chasing a scorpion! It had spotted one that was scurrying under a rock to seek shelter from the midday heat.

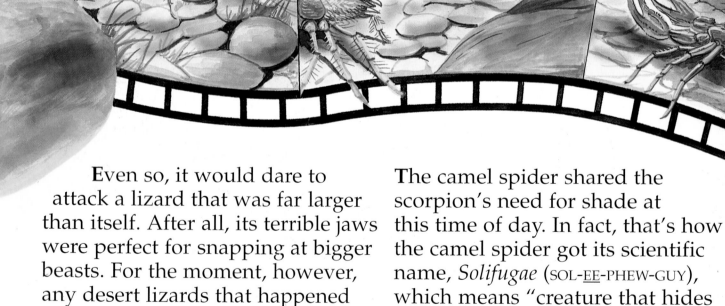

Even so, it would dare to attack a lizard that was far larger than itself. After all, its terrible jaws were perfect for snapping at bigger beasts. For the moment, however, any desert lizards that happened to be close by were safe.

The camel spider shared the scorpion's need for shade at this time of day. In fact, that's how the camel spider got its scientific name, *Solifugae* (SOL-EE-PHEW-GUY), which means "creature that hides from the sun."

16

the death

The near-sighted scorpion had not noticed the predator's approach. It merely sensed some vibrations. It mistakenly thought the vibrations came from a creature that would provide nourishment. So it ventured slowly from its hiding place.

At once, they began to spar, just as human boxers do. The camel spider instinctively knew that it had to attack where the true danger lay. Viciously, it bit the scorpion's tail and severed its stinger.

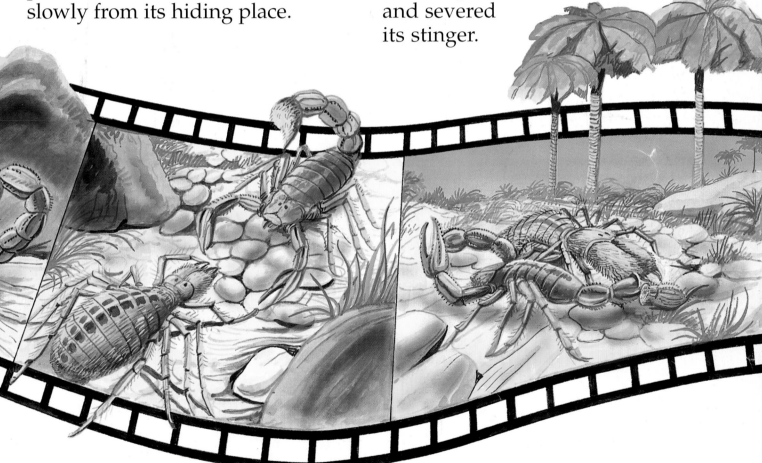

It now came face to face with the eight-legged camel spider.

For the scorpion, it was all over. The camel spider had won.

Myths and

Some people once believed that, if cornered by an enemy, the scorpion would take its own life with its stinger. This is because the stinger is sometimes bent so far back over the scorpion's body that it really does look as if it might be stinging itself. But this is only a myth.

According to folklore, the scorpion carried an oil that could be used to cure its own sting. But no one has been able to prove this yet.

If your birthday falls between October 23 and November 22, you were born under Scorpio, a zodiac sign named after the scorpion. There is a legend that Orion, a hunter, boasted he could track and kill any living creature. He could not fight off a scorpion, however, which attacked and stung him fatally in the heel.

legends

Tradition has it that Orion, the hunter, was later brought back to life and placed in the heavens. The scorpion, too, was given a place in the skies, where it became known as Scorpio. It was positioned opposite the constellation of Orion, so that the two would never have to confront each other again.

Another old legend tells us that the scorpion will sting itself to death if it is completely surrounded by a ring of fire, but no evidence of this has ever been found.

Finally, the scorpion's sting is so painful that the name *scorpion* was given to a medieval whip with steel spikes, used as a terrible form of punishment. This scorpion whip was probably more deadly than the creature itself.

Scorpions by

▼ Some animals that have the word *scorpion* as part of their name are not actually related to the *true* scorpion. Among these are the scorpion flies, which have existed since prehistoric times. They were given this name because their genital organs look like the stinger of a true scorpion. Scorpion flies are not venomous, however. They live in Europe and North America, mainly in woodlands and hedges.

▲ Scorpion fish are so-called because, just like the true scorpion, they can be extremely venomous — even fatal at times — to humans. They store venom in some of their spines. If you ever go swimming in tropical waters, you'll need to keep an eye out for the approach of scorpion fish. Be careful not to disturb them if you spot any! Some scorpion fish grow to 3 feet (1 meter) in length, which is longer than your arm.

name only

▼ **W**hip scorpions, like the one *below*, have some characteristics in common with true scorpions. For example, they are nocturnal hunters and do not like light. One type has a long, thin tail, or "whip," at the end of its abdomen. It also has claws for catching prey, which it will then crush. Another type has no tail but long "whips" for legs. Whip scorpions do not sting but can secrete a substance that will cause intense irritation. Whip scorpions usually walk sideways, like a crab, rather than forward or backward like most other animals.

▲ False scorpions are distantly related to true scorpions but do not have a stinger and are only about 1/2 inch (1 cm) long. They usually make their homes under stones or in rotting vegetation. One type, the book scorpion, crawls around in the pages of old books. False scorpions can travel backward as well as forward. Others use another form of transportation. They hitch rides on flying insects by grabbing the insects' legs and then hanging on for dear life as they take to the air.

Did you know?

Are scorpions insects?
For a living creature to be called an insect, it has to have six legs. Instead, scorpions belong to a class that scientists call *arachnids*, all of which have eight legs. Spiders and mites are other members of the arachnid class.

▼ Is it true that scorpions sometimes glow in the dark?
Scorpions have a substance on their bodies that will glow under ultraviolet light. If scientists need scorpion specimens, they will sometimes search for them by the light of an ultraviolet lamp. This makes the scorpions shine a greenish yellow, which makes them easy to spot.

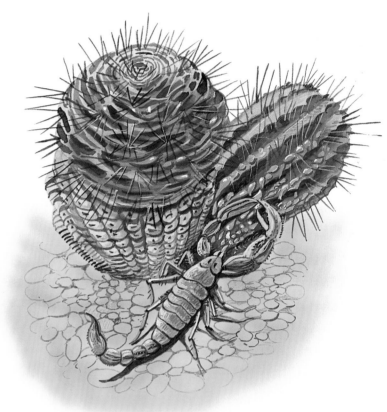

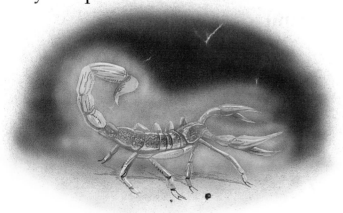

▲ Do scorpions drink?
Scorpions can go without water for several months. This is important, since so many of them live in desert conditions. Scorpions get most of the liquid their bodies need from the insects and other creatures they eat. But they do actually drink water from time to time and will also drink the morning dew.

Why do scorpions sing, and what does it mean?

Some types of scorpions make a "singing" noise by rubbing the bottom of their claws against the first pair of legs they use for walking. They make this sound when ready to attack, as a threat to the enemy.

▼ Is it true that scorpions are cannibals?

Just as they can survive without water for a long time, scorpions can also survive without food for months. But if they get extremely hungry, the larger ones may try to eat the rest. Once, two hundred scorpions were left alone in a cage for a while. Eventually, there was just one severely overweight live scorpion surrounded by the remains of all the others.

▲ Is it true that scorpions like fire?

Scorpions may be attracted to the glow of a camp fire, just as moths are attracted to an electric light or the flame of a candle. So when sleeping or cooking outdoors in regions where scorpions are known to live, keep a careful watch out for them. And be sure all camp fires are completely extinguished after use. Fires spread very easily and quickly.

Do scorpions have enemies?

Lizards, some birds, snakes, and baboons — all can be enemies of the scorpion.

23

Glossary

abdomen — the back part of the scorpion's body (behind the thorax) that contains the stomach.

cannibal — an animal that feeds on others of its own kind.

carnivore — a meat-eater.

constellation — a group of stars.

fatal — causing death.

nocturnal — active at night. Scorpions are nocturnal hunters.

pincers — special jointed body parts that help certain animals grasp their prey.

thorax — the middle section, or chest cavity, of an animal that holds the heart and lungs.

ultraviolet light — a type of light that has shorter wavelengths than ordinary light. It can kill some forms of bacteria, but too much exposure to it can be harmful to humans.

venomous — poisonous.

Books and Videos

Scorpion. Jan Mell (Macmillan)

Scorpion Man: Exploring the World of Scorpions. Laurence Pringle (Macmillan)

Scorpions. Walter Myers (HarperCollins)

Scorpions. Conrad Storad (Lerner)

Scorpion. (Coronet video)

Snakes, Scorpions, and Spiders. (Learning Corporation of America video)

Index